Start Strong © 2024 Terrence Thomas. All Rights Reserved

No portion of the book form or by any means photocopy, recording by anyone but the publisher not be reproduced in any form without the written permission of the publisher, except by a reviewer who wishes to quote brief passage in connection with a review written for inclusion in a magazine or newspaper and has written approval prior to publishing.

For information contact:
Terrence Thomas Brands
Email:
golf@terrencethomas.com
website: www.maximumgolf.net

Warning – Disclaimer

The workouts and other health-related activities described in this book were developed by the author and are to be used as an adjunct to improved strength, conditioning, health and ftness. These programs may not be appropriate for everyone. All individuals, especially those who sufer from any disease or are recovering from an injury of any sort, should consult their physician regarding the advisability of undertaking any of the activities suggested in these programs. The author has been diligent in his research. However he is neither responsible nor liable for any harm or injury resulting from this program or the use of the exercises or exercise devices described herein.

PREFACE

PREFACE:

Let me tell you a tale of two golfers. No, this isn't some ancient parable passed down from the legendary fairways of yore, but rather a modern-day story that perfectly illustrates why you've picked up this book. Meet Gary and Ben.

Gary, bless his heart, is the quintessential weekend warrior. He loves the game, truly he does. But Jerry's idea of warming up consists of a quick wiggle, a giggle, and a half-hearted practice swing that looks more like he's swatting a particularly pesky fly. He's the guy you see sprinting from his car, golf shoes half-tied, with a donut in one hand and a coffee in the other, arriving at the first tee with just enough time to wave at his buddies and say, "Let's do this!"

Then there's Ben. Ben approaches golf with the discipline and precision of a samurai monk. He arrives early, his clubs meticulously arranged, and spends a good half-hour going through his warm-up routine. He stretches, practices his breathing, and performs drills with the focus of someone about to enter an epic showdown. Ben understands that the first tee shot sets the tone for the entire round, and he's determined to be ready.

So, what happens when these two meet on the course? Gary's first drive, fueled by caffeine and optimism, slices hard right, barely missing the neighboring fairway. Ben, on the other hand, steps up with the calm confidence of a Zen master and sends his ball soaring straight down the middle. By the time they reach the second hole, Gary's already muttering under his breath, while Ben is serenely planning his next shot.

Now, don't get me wrong. We love Gary's enthusiasm and carefree spirit. But if you're reading this book, chances are you're looking to add a bit more Ben to your game. You see, a proper warm-up isn't just about physical preparation; it's about setting the mental stage for a great round of golf. It's about starting strong and saving strokes right from the first tee.

In the pages that follow, I'll show you a proven routine that has worked consistently since I introduced it to golfers back in 2006. From head control drills to shoulder turn exercises, from swing plane mastery to hip coil techniques, and rotational mobility routines, you'll find everything you need to approach the first tee with confidence and precision.

PREFACE:

Let's leave the quick wiggles and giggles to Gary. By the time you're done with this book, you'll have a new found skill set and deep respect for the pre-golf warmup. You'll have your new competitive advantage hiding in your golf bag waiting to serve you at any time. Let's start strong and make every round your best round yet.

Hit it long and putt it true,

Terrence

INTRODUCTION

MECHANICS ABOVE ALL ELSE

Do you know the #1 reason why most golfers lose distance and accuracy in their golf swing?

Do you know the #1 reason why most golfers lose distance and accuracy and play to their full potential?

- Is it an injury?
- Poor club fitting?
- Lack of instruction?
- How about age?

The reality is that ALL of these can kill your golf swing, but here is the real problem that you face...

When you can't make a proper golf swing move, your body starts to compensate.

To fix this, your brain starts to make your body do some very bad things. Things like...

- Trying to hit the ball farther by swinging harder, which means that you will lose more distance because trying to swing harder creates extra body tension. As world famous PGA Instructor Jim Mclean says, "tension kills the golf swing".

- When you swing too hard, it will cause your lower back to hurt, which means you will now have to compensate because you are in pain.

- If your back hurts, you can't make a full back swing from your core and hips, so you compensate by pulling more with your arms.

Now! you are forced to get extra "handsy" on your downswing and follow through, because you can't use the big muscles to generate torque, which means you lose even more club head speed and distance off the tee.

After repeating these habits for several hundred strokes, now your shoulder, elbow and wrist start to hurt. At this point your whole body is compensating to make a proper golf move and it gets worse every time you try to play.

Now here's the bad news. No amount of golf lessons, expensive new golf clubs and fancy gadgets will fix any of this. Sounds terrible right?

Where do you begin to add more distance and accuracy when you can't make a proper golf swing move? This question is exactly why you are reading this book and will get the answers as you read on.

Start Strong is a program that trains your body how to make the proper golf moves from head to toe. The techniques that you're about to learn will be the foundation to your developing a powerful, consistent and injury resistant golf swing.

WARNING: To get maximum results, it's best to follow the plan EXACTY as I have designed it. There is a time for imitation and a time for innovation. As your coach, the first concept that I want to share with you is F.T.D.I. This is a powerful acronym that learned, and it means (Follow The Darn Instructions). Now is your time to imitate the drills as they are shown. Once you are proficient, then you can entertain the idea of adding a little extra to your routine. If you do decide to sprinkle a little your own sauce, you'll learn your second important concept. These techniques are evergreen and will work for you all day and every day. I have used these techniques for the last 22 years and they have worked without fail for myself as well as over 15,000 other golfers.

Just like the golf swing itself, it's all about the details. If you take your time and approach each drill with patience and purpose, you will literally rebuild your golf swing mechanics from the ground up. You will become the walking example of how small improvements in the way your body moves will lead to large improvements on the golf course. Does that sound like a plan? Fantastic! Onward and upward.

FINAL WARNING: This book must be read fully and the program carried out properly. It's no good skimming the pages, trying one stretch, and then deciding it doesn't work. We all have the natural ability to add lots of distance to our swings, but it takes time to build up the power. So relax, read every section, follow the plans, then get out on the course and watch your friends ask "how do you drive like that?!"

INTRODUCTION

THE FOUNDATION OF A WINNING GOLF SWING

A big mistake that I see even the best players in the world make is they start to play "whack a mole" with these 3 aspects of their game. Tiger Woods is a perfect example. The golf swing mechanics that he had when he won his first block of major championships was a swing for the ages. Why do I say this? Because his power, distance, accuracy, and stats proved it. It was only when Tiger's swing lost its triple threat is when the field caught up to him. When Tiger was super focused on adding more power, is accuracy and consistency suffered. It also was so accident that this is when he started to suffer more injuries as well.

My reason for this story is that I am a GIANT fan of Tiger and it's still my goal to work with him. I am one million percent confident that if I had been his golf performance coach, he would have 20 majors right now. I say this because when you have the raw natural talent like Tiger, all that is needed is to keep building a stronger foundation. Here's what I mean
Golf swing power, accuracy and consistency require that you stack a specific set of skills and in the correct order. When you stack these skills in the right order and at the right time you, can will your golf swing bullet proof. **The skills that you must stack are Flexibility, Mobility, Balance, Strength and Power.** (See Figure below)

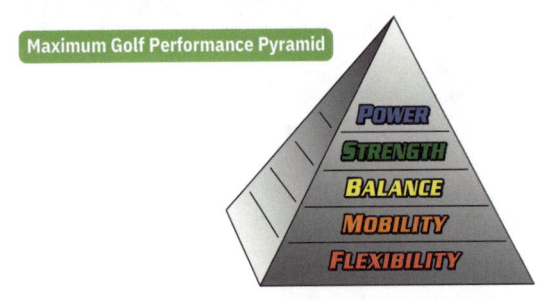

Maximum Golf Performance Pyramid

Tiger confirmed this approach in an interview when he said, "You can swing as hard as you want, provided you have the balance and control to do it.". Stacking skills is how you do it, and **Start Strong** is your path to making it happen. Let's get started.

Your coach,
Terrence

PHASE I
FLEXIBILITY

PHASE I: FLEXIBILITY

- POWER
- STRENGTH
- BALANCE
- MOBILITY
- *FLEXIBILITY*

HOW TO ACCESS YOUR HIDDEN POWER

Many of my clients are amazed at how their ball striking improves when they master the art of corrective stretching. Flexibility is the gatekeeper to starting your round of golf strong. In other words, your ability to keep your swing on plane (accuracy) and generate club head speed (power) will only be as good as your flexibility and mobility and here's why.

> **Start Strong Principle #1**
> A tight muscle is a weak muscle

Have you ever tried to lift a weight that you thought you could lift only for your body to totally freeze up only to gather yourself, focus and then actually lift the weight? Here's what happened with that...

On your first attempt, your inhibition reflexes weren't turned on and on the second attempt they were turned off. There are stretch receptors in your muscles that prevent you from hurting yourself. When you attempt your golf swing and your body is not ready, muscles that should fire either don't fire or they fire at the wrong time. We call this poor body mechanics.

For example, a tight hip muscle will restrict hip mechanics during the golf swing. The tighter the hip muscle gets, the weaker it gets. Tightness begets weakness and weakness begets tightness. It's a perpetuating cycle that will continue until the muscle is properly stretched and balanced. A properly executed stretch will tell the body that it is safe to relax – as such releasing the body's parking brake. This is the essence of "pliability" and flexibility.

HOW TO ACCESS YOUR HIDDEN POWER

Have you ever tried to lift a weight that you thought you could lift only for your body to totally freeze up only to gather yourself, focus and then actually lift the weight? Here's what happened with that…
On your first attempt, your inhibition reflexes weren't turned on and on the second attempt they were turned off. There are stretch receptors in your muscles that prevent you from hurting yourself. When you attempt your golf swing and your body is not ready, muscles that should fire either don't fire or they fire at the wrong time. We call this poor body mechanics.
For example, a tight hip muscle will restrict hip mechanics during the golf swing. The tighter the hip muscle gets, the weaker it gets. Tightness begets weakness and weakness begets tightness. It's a perpetuating cycle that will continue until the muscle is properly stretched and balanced. A properly executed stretch will tell the body that it is safe to relax – as such releasing the body's parking brake. This is the essence of "pliability" and flexibility.

> **Start Strong Principle #2**
> Compensation Patterns Block Golf Swing Potential

The golf swing is a one-sided movement therefore, the body will develop imbalances on the dominant side. Right-handed players will get shorter on the right side and lefties on the left. When you add in the damaging effects of sitting, it becomes more of a challenge to build a powerful, accurate and consistent swing while remaining injury free. Sedentary posture and the one-sided nature of the golf swing make it mandatory for any golfer to have a routine in place to keep the body in balance and free of restrictions. Not having a routine in place puts your golf swing at risk. Muscle imbalances literally hijack your mechanics one small degree at a time. For every degree that you lose in one area, the body
tries to make up for it in another. The more you swing the club while compensating, the more difficult it is to break the compensation pattern. Unless you retune your body with corrective stretching.

HOW TO STRETCH FOR POWER, ACCURACY & CONSISTENCY

Start Stronger is designed in stages so that you progress through your levels of conditioning by stacking skills in the right order. Your golf conditioning program can be compared to building a pyramid in that it must have a solid foundation. The foundation is built upon **flexibility** and **mobility.**

> **Start Strong Principle #3**
> Muscle Balance and Flexibility as well as Static and Dynamic Stability (balance) control 80% of ball fight factors
> (Paul Chek)

Two important notes before we begin:

1. Stretching is more than just sticking your leg out or trying to touch your toes.

There are specific techniques that will convert a "normal" stretch into a body transforming experience. With that said, please approach your stretching drills with the utmost attention. Pay attention to the written instructions as each stretch will have a key relaxation tip that will increase flexibility very quickly. Just like your golf swing, it will take practice to master all of the drills in this program. It will be time well spent when you are on the golf course feeling fresh and strong while your opponents are looking like the Hunchback of Notre Dame at the end of the round!

2. Breathing technique is vital to maximizing your stretching exercises

All breathing should be done through the diaphragm. As you inhale through your nose, your belly and lower ribs should expand and your upper chest and neck should remain very relaxed.

WARNING! Many of the stretching techniques require that you hold your breath slightly while increasing pressure in your trunk. If you have a medical condition that prevents you from holding your breath, please consult your doctor before starting this program.

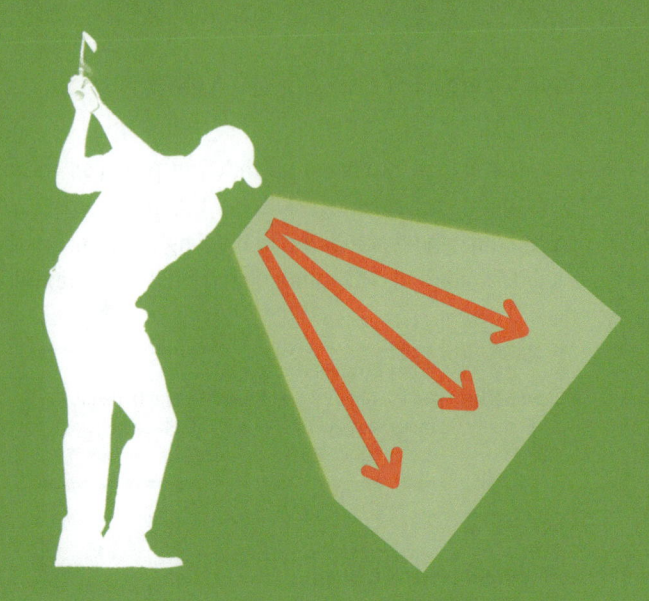

SECTION I:
HEAD CONTROL

Head Control Drills

1. Head Rotation

TARGET AREA: Neck rotators
BENEFITS: Improved neck mobility and shoulder turn. Neck mobility will allow the head to remain steady during all phases of the golf swing – this can translate into improved shot accuracy, consistency, and distance.

Instructions

1. Stand with your feet parallel and at shoulder width.

2. Place your hand fat on your left cheek.

3. Turn head to the right as far as comfortably possible.

4. Take a deep breath through your nose.

5. Hold your breath in and gently press your cheek against your hand as if to turn your head back to the left, but not actually moving.

6. Fully exhale through your mouth and move further into the stretch. When you
exhale allow the air to escape naturally. Do not blow the air out. Simply relax and exhale through and open and relaxed mouth.

7. You will not move very far on this stretch. Simply focus on creating relaxation.

PROGRESSION:

If you are able to rotate your head 90 degrees i.e. chin over shoulder, you can progress into a maintenance phase with this stretch.

Maintenance means that you will do the stretch to maintain current flexibility rather than to increase it. Maintenance typically calls for doing a stretch for 1 to 2 reps after exercise or playing. If you have a physical limitation that prevents you from achieving full range of motion, simply use your judgment as to how far you will turn your head.

START STRONG

2. Neck Side Bend

TARGET AREA: Side flexors of the neck, upper respiratory muscles

BENEFITS: Increased control of head shift on the back swing that will translate to better shot accuracy and angle of attack.

Instructions

1. Stand with your feet parallel and at shoulder width.
2. Bring your left ear to your left shoulder. Do not lift your shoulder towards your ear.
3. Provide assistance with your left hand. Gently pull your head closer to your shoulder.
4. From this new position inhale, hold your breath and gently press your head against your hand as if to try to bring your head back to the upright position but not actually moving.
5. Exhale through your mouth and fall deeper into the stretch.
6. Like the head rotation stretch you will not move very far. Simply focus on the relaxation after you exhale.
7. Perform 2-3 relaxation breaths on each side.

PROGRESSION: Normal range of motion for the neck side bend is about 45 degrees or about the 2 o'clock position.

3. Levator Scapulae Stretch

TARGET AREA: Levator Scapulae – the bridge between the neck and shoulder

BENEFITS: Allows for a full backswing; helps relieve neck tension. Do you slice the ball? Lose a lot of power? Constantly push/shank your shot? This stretch can really help. The levator scapulae stretch is a combination of the head rotation and neck side bend. It is true that all muscles are important for optimal golf performance but there are some that can really cause problems and the levator scapulae muscle is one of them.

The levator scapulae connect to the shoulders and neck so it can affect your head control and shoulder turn. From the neck it could affect your ability to keep your eye on the ball by causing your head to tilt. Since your head is like a gyroscope in that the eyes always want stay level with the horizon, a head tilt will cause your eyes to compensate and may lead to imbalances in the eye muscles later. This may be important to you if want to avoid burying yourself alive in a sand trap because you keep missing the ball. At the shoulder, the levator scapulae muscle will restrict your backswing and cause you to lose power, slice, push the ball, hit a shank or all of the above. If you have a problem with this muscle, this stretch will help the problem.

Instructions

1. Place your right hand behind your head with fingers facing down. Keep elbow up shoulders pressed down.
2. Turn your head to the left and grab the back of your head with your left hand
3. Gently pull your head down towards your left collar bone.
4. From this end position take a deep breath, hold it and then gently press the
back of your head against your hand like you are trying to lift your head but not actually moving.
5. Stop pushing with your head, exhale through the mouth and relax further into the stretch.

PHASE I: FLEXIBILITY

PROGRESSION: The levator scapulae muscle is tricky in that it can sometimes actually be too loose. You have to go by feel. If your chin sinks down way past your collar bone and do not feel a good pull when you are in position, then perform this stretch for maintenance only – the wall lean exercise that you will learn in the Balance phase of this program will be more beneficial for you.

At the shoulder, the levator scapulae muscle will restrict your backswing and cause you to lose power, slice, push, hit a shank or all of the above.

SECTION II:
SHOULDER TURN

4. Trunk Side Bend Stretch

TARGET AREA: Side flexors of the trunk
BENEFITS: Stops main cause of power leak in the golf swing; Maintains body alignment and posture, promoting a smooth backswing and follow-through.

The focus of the trunk side bend is to release the close relative of the levator scapulae – the quadratus lumborum (QLO). This muscle gets tight because of the repeated contractions at the impact position of the golf swing. For right handed golfers the right QLO will become tight and the left one for lefties.

In my opinion, the QLO is even nastier than the levator scapulae muscle because the fibers are much denser making it very difficult to stretch!

A tight QLO will cause your shoulder on the same side to drop down, lock your hip in place preventing you from coiling and uncoiling your hips. This will cause a MAJOR POWER LEAK in your swing.

Being a manual therapist I can give you a first hand account of the misery that people endure to get this muscle fixed. If you do trunk side bend stretches regularly, it will save you the misery of having someone dig into your low back with an elbow or some other blunt object!

4. Trunk Side Bend Stretch -continued

Instructions

1. Stand with feet shoulder width apart.
2. Keep knees locked and squeeze buttocks.
3. Bend to the left and imagine you are sliding along an imaginary wall. If you
cannot feel the stretch in your side just above your hip bone, you will most likely
need to place your back against a real wall.
4. The left arm is along the side of the left leg. The right arm is reaching overhead.
5. Take a deep breath in, hold for a second while tightening your butt, thighs and
fsts. Imagine that you are returning back to the upright position but not actually
moving. Just contract your side muscles like you are trying to. Finally exhale
through your mouth sinking further into the stretch.
6. Lift both arms overhead to increase the intensity of the stretch. Lower your
right arm to make the stretch easier.
7. Perform the same sequence on the opposite side.

START STRONG

PROGRESSION: You will need to use your own judgment in determining your need for the side bend stretch. Since the quadratus lumborum muscle is being tightened with every golf swing, it's my opinion that this stretch will remain in your routine indefinitely!

This is the muscle that contracts very forcefully at the impact point on the downswing and at the finish of the golf swing.

5. Thoracic Mobilization

TARGET AREA: Thoracic spine and upper abdominals
BENEFITS: Loosens the upper back to allow for easier rotation and a smooth backswing. Range of motion in the thoracic spine is paramount for a good golf swing! I cannot stress that enough.

For every degree that the spine cannot rotate, the shoulder joint will compensate accordingly. Restricted rotation will cause you to use your arms rather than your body, which will lead to all sorts of swing problems, from loss of distance to shots with zero accuracy. This problem typically shows up as wrist and elbow tendonitis.

Instructions

1. Fold a normal sized bath towel in half lengthwise twice.
2. Lay the towel on the floor and roll the towel half way up.
3. Sit in front of the roll with the fat side up towards your head.
4. Lie down over the towel with the roll under your upper back. A good starting place for the towel is just below your shoulder blades.
5. Place your hands behind your head and allow your elbows to touch the floor. If this position is uncomfortable for your shoulder, extend your arms straight out to the side.
6. Take deep breaths to allow the rib cage to expand and contract. Your belly should rise and fall with each breath.
7. Take 3 deep breaths and move the rolled portion of the towel up towards your head about 2 inches. Repeat 3 breaths then move the towel up one more time.
8. Repeat the cycle by starting below the shoulder blades.

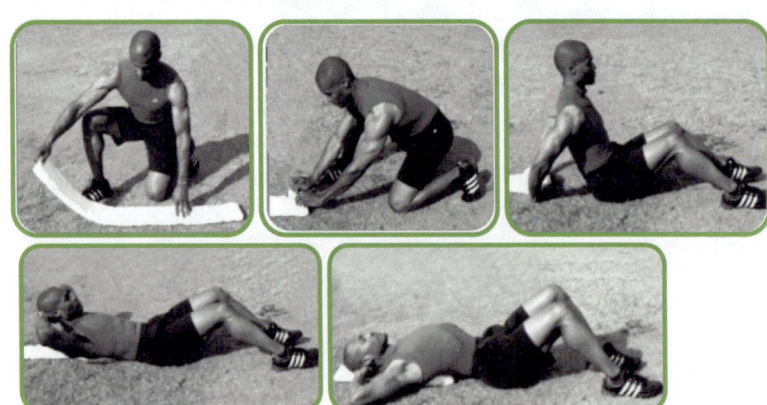

6. Kneeling Back Twist

TARGET AREA: Thoracic spine and shoulder girdle
BENEFITS: Improves rotation in the golf swing; Improves flexibility and range of motion.

The kneeling back twist is the second piece to loosening up the thoracic spine. Thoracic mobilizations address the extension of the spine and the back twist coves the rotational aspect of the swing.

Instructions

1. Kneel on all-fours with your buttocks touching your heels.
2. Place your hands shoulder width apart and keep your elbows turned in (i.e. your biceps facing forward).
3. Lift your right arm and extend it behind your body. The thumb side of your hand is facing up.
4. VERY IMPORTANT! Extend your arm back only as far as your body will allow. Forcing your arm back will upset your shoulder and reinforce a bad movement pattern.
5. Once you have rotated back as far as you can, hold this position.
6. Take a deep breath and hold it for 2 seconds, then exhale trying to rotate a bit more.
7. Do this release technique 2 more times, then change sides.

7. Shoulder Twist

TARGET AREA: Spinal rotators, shoulder and upper back muscles

BENEFITS: Discourages "fat hits"; Encourages more flexibility and mobility in the backswing

The shoulder twist will assist you with your backswing, as it releases the brakes on the muscles that twist the spine and in the upper back, and allows your lead arm to cross your chest easier.

TIP! This is a good stretch to do in the middle of your round. If you find yourself hitting it fat (making large divots) the shoulder twist opposite of your backswing may help. So if you are right handed, perform a shoulder twist to the left.

Instructions

1. Stand with your feet shoulder width apart and knees slightly bent
2. Pull your left arm across your body with the palm facing upward. Keep your left arm straight
3. From this position keep your head fixed and then rotate your body to the right as far as possible.
4. Keep your legs straight, buttocks tight and hips square as you turn your shoulders
5. Take a deep breath and hold it for a second. At the same time push your left arm into your right hand but do not move. Focus on turning your torso back to the left without actually moving. Hold this position for a second and then release and twist further into the stretch (i.e. back to the right). You may not move very far. Simply focus on relaxing after you exhale using the breathing techniques discussed earlier
6. Advance this drill by combining it with a bend

PROGRESSION: Stretch the tight shoulder until you have equal twisting action on both sides.

START STRONG

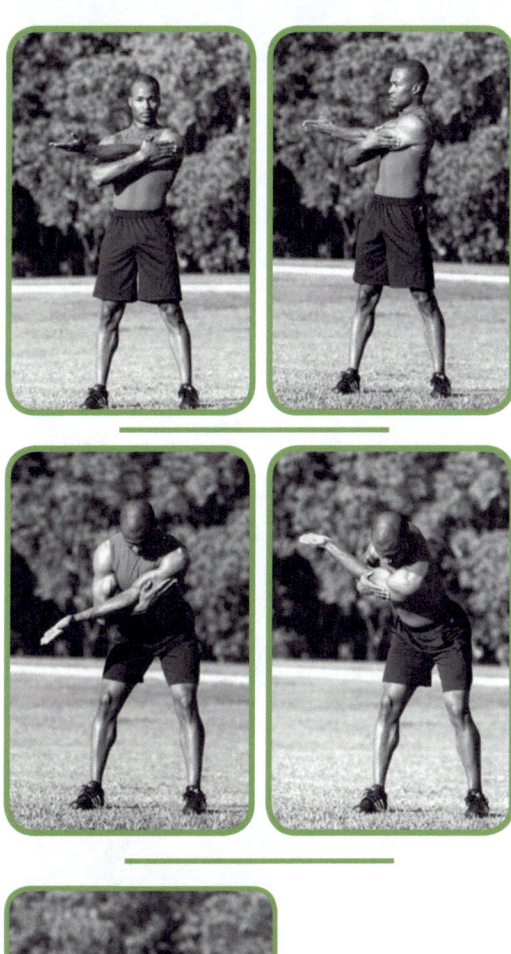

If you fnd yourself "hitting it fat" (making large divots) the shoulder twist opposite of your backswing may help.

SECTION III:
SWING PLANE

8. Good Morning Stretch

TARGET AREA: Hamstrings
BENEFITS: Increased swing power; Hamstring flexibility, hip and lower back mobility.

If your idea of a "good morning" is splitting the fairway with a long drive, then this stretch will certainly help! The skill of folding from the hips is vital to a smooth, powerful and safe golf swing. In addition to releasing tight hamstrings, the Good Morning stretch is the first drill that will teach you the skill of the hip fold.

The hamstrings are important to golf because tight hamstrings will restrict your ability to bend. If you have tight hamstrings, they will lock your hips into place forcing the lower back to compensate by bending more. This will most definitely spell disaster for your lower back (and golf swing!) if not corrected.

Instructions

1. Stand with your feet parallel and about hip width apart.
2. Bend your knees slightly.
3. Bend forward by folding from the hips. If you have trouble with the hip fold, place your hands in the crease of your hips. If your back starts to hurt as you bend, use support from the back of a chair or golf cart until you can fold at the hip more efficiently. If you have a good hip fold, you can have both hands in front.
4. Keep your head up, breastbone lifted and tailbone lifted
5. Keep the lower back straight and only go down as far as you can keep it straight.
6. Once you have reached the sticking point in the stretch, take a deep breath in and hold it. Then squeeze your buttocks and abdominals for a second. It will almost feel like you are going to the bathroom but holding it in at the same time!
7. Exhale through your mouth, release your buttocks, abdominals and then sink further into the stretch.

PROGRESSION: The normal bend position for the Good Morning stretch is about 50 degrees. If you can bend forward as far as the illustration while keeping the lower back straight, you are ready for the maintenance phase of your flexibility program.

PHASE I: FLEXIBILITY

If you have tight hamstrings, they will lock your hips into place forcing the lower back to compensate by bending more. This will most definitely spell disaster for your lower back if not corrected.

9. Cigarette Butt Stretch

TARGET AREA: Hip Rotators (Primary), Hamstrings (Secondary)
BENEFITS: Hip coordination in the swing; Hip rotator flexibility and mobility.

The cigarette butt stretch is adopted from the _Golf Biomechanics Manual_ and addresses hip flexibility, mobility and coordination. It adds a rotation component to the hip fold and simulates the hip mechanics of the golf swing. The cigarette butt stretches the piriformis muscle that sits under the meaty gluteus maximus and acts as its little helper. Unfortunately most people's buttocks are weak and, as a result, the piriformis works harder than it needs to.

The proof is in the increasing number of lower back injuries. A strong gluteus maximus will protect the pelvis and lower back from injury. You will learn how to build a powerful set of buttocks in the power development series of the Maximum Golf Performance Curriculum

Instructions

1. Stand with your feet parallel and shoulder width apart
2. Lift your right toe in the air and then turn it in about 45 degrees to the left

3. Shift your weight back toward your right heel while folding at the hip. Place your right hand in the crease of your right hip if you are having trouble. You should now feel the stretch in your right buttock. The key is to kick the hip out to the right.
4. At this point take a deep breath in and hold it. Then squeeze your buttocks and abdominals for a second.
5. Exhale through your mouth, release your buttocks and abdominals, then sink further into the stretch. Keep your lower back straight tail bone up like in the Good Morning stretch.

PHASE I: FLEXIBILITY

PROGRESSION: This is another stretch you will need to go by feel. If you get into the correct position and do not feel significant tightness, progress to maintenance.

34

10. Windmill Stretch

TARGET AREA: Hamstrings, spine rotators, hip rotators
BENEFITS: All round golf flexibility and rotational mobility; Chest opener; Low level strength and stability.

The windmill stretch is an integrative posture that combines the skills of the bend, hip fold, and trunk twist patterns of the golf swing. It combines the skills learned in the Good Morning and Cigarette Butt stretches. Mastery of this drill will download some great software into your nervous system, that will upgrade your golf performance in a nanosecond.

Instructions
1. Stand with your feet parallel and shoulder width apart.
2. Lift your toes in the air and turn them to the right about 45 degrees.

3. Place your right hand in the crease of your right hip. Now kick your hip out to the left.
4. Bend forward in the direction of your toes. Bend at the hips focusing on increasing the hip crease.
5. Reach above your head with your left arm. Push your arm slightly behind your body.
6. Look up at your left hand.
7. Keep the left shoulder pressed down by squeezing the armpit of your left arm. This squeezing of the armpit will be important in the kettlebell military press, windmill and bent press strength exercises. How do you squeeze your armpit? Do this by pressing your shoulder down towards your hips.

PHASE I: FLEXIBILITY

8. Breathe in and squeeze your buttocks, and abdominals. Exhale, release and sink down further into the windmill

9. To increase the rotation, pretend like you are pressing against an imaginary wall with your left hand trying to twist your body back to the left

PROGRESSION: The windmill stretch is an integrative stretch that combines two key components of the golf swing. Therefore I recommend that it is performed indefinitely.

SECTION IV:
HIP COIL

11. Groin Rock Stretch

TARGET AREA: Short adductors

BENEFITS: Ideal hip posture and mobility in the hips. This allows for greater control over the body and therefore the golf swing itself.

Since all movement emanates from the core or center of the body, hip mobility equals better body control and better body control equals more accurate and powerful golf shots!

And this doozie will definitely have you crying for mommy, especially if theses muscles are tight – and they are in most people!

The short adductor muscles are dense, thick and get tight very easily. The Groin Rock Stretch will give you some added freedom in your hips to further release the power breaks in your hips.

Instructions

1. Kneel on the floor with a towel or mat under your knees.
2. Spread your knees apart as far as you can and rest your weight on your forearms.
3. Your toes are pointed outward like a frog.
4. Shift your hips back towards your feet while keeping an arch in your lower back i.e. stick your butt out. Only go back as far as you can keep your butt out.
5. Now from this position take a deep breath in and hold it. Now squeeze your inner thighs into the floor and hold for three to five seconds.
6. Exhale and relax further into the stretch. You may not open your legs very far after you exhale. Simply focus on relaxing into the stretch
7. Move into the recovery position for a few seconds then repeat the sequence. If these muscles are tight you will soon know why it is a "recovery" position!

11. Groin Rock Stretch

PROGRESSION: Some muscles will unfortunately always be tight and the inner thigh muscles are one of them. Most women and very flexible men will have a tendency to loosen up quickly with this stretch and may need to go into a maintenance phase once they have adequately stretched these muscles. But for the rest of us, the groin rock stretch will be a part of our flexibility program indefinitely.

12. Kneeling Lunge Stretch

TARGET AREA: Hip flexors
BENEFITS: Can help protect the lower back during the golf swing; Restores mobility and flexibility in the hips and spine.

The hip flexors are the muscular link between the spine and the legs. Doctor Vladimir Janda, an international authority on rehabilitation, states that most muscle imbalances originate at the hip flexors. He is saying that the hip flexors affect the posture of the upper and lower body.

Tight hip flexors will place extra compression forces on your lower back. If you combine these forces with the forces generated during the golf swing, tight hip flexors have the potential to create a very serious injury to the lower back. If you do have tight hip flexors, the kneeling lunge stretch will help.

Instructions

1. Kneel on the floor in the lunge position. Start with your left knee down.
2. Your arms are at your sides.
3. Lift your chest and squeeze your shoulder blades together.
4. Tuck your tail under, squeeze your buttocks and then lean forward by pushing your hips forward. 80% of your weight is on your front foot.
5. Keep both feet planted solidly on the floor. Pretend that you are trying to split the floor open by pushing your front foot and back knee in opposite directions.
6. Take a deep breath in. Hold the air in your lungs for a second. At the same time, apply more pressure to your "split the floor" technique.
7. Exhale through the mouth and then relax further into the stretch.

INTERMEDIATE VERSION: Place your left arm overhead and your left hand on your left hip

ADVANCED VERSION: Place your right hand on the floor and rotate more

PROGRESSION: The hip flexors are a bit tricky in that they tend to be really tight or really loose. Either scenario can produce posture imbalances and or back pain.

START STRONG

A dead giveaway that you have *tight hip flexors* is that you have a *Donald Duck posture* in your hips i.e. your butt sticks out excessively. On the other hand if you have a Pink Panther type posture – where your hips project forward in relation to your shoulders – you most likely have loose hip flexors. If you perform the lunge stretch with proper form and do not feel the stretch deep in the groin area you may have loose hip flexors and will need to go to maintenance mode with the lunge stretch.

Arms down

KNEELING LUNGE STRETCH (INTERMEDIATE)

Arm Up on Active Side

PHASE I: FLEXIBILITY

KNEELING LUNGE STRETCH (ADVANCED)

Hand Touches Ground

Active Hand Behind Head

PHASE II
MOBILITY & BODY CONTROL

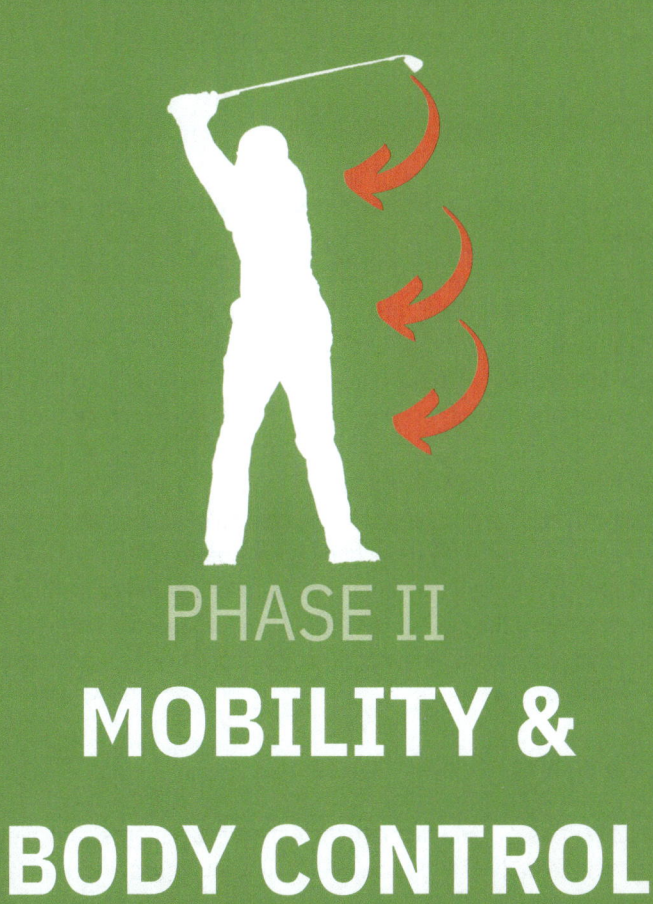

RELAX...RECHARGE...REPEAT!

Start Strong Mobility Drills: Develop command over your new flexibility

How did NFL quarterback Tom Brady continue to perform at such a high level despite being in his mid 40's? It's because he understands the concept of mobility. His TB12 method calls it "pliability" but this concept is falls under phase II of the The Triple Threat Golf Swing method.

Research has shown that the golf swing requires about 90% of voluntary muscular effort. That means you use almost all of your available power when swinging a golf club. If the body is not prepared for such an effort, you will greatly increase your chances of getting injured or not playing at your best because the inhibition reflexes in your muscles in are still activated. In other words the more ready you are to play, you'll play better.

The Drills in this section will help you:

- Quickly increase circulation to the muscles, ligaments, and joints.
- Relieve the body of any excess tension from nerves or chronically tight muscles.
- Prime the fast twitch muscles and nervous system to make a good golf move from the first tee.
- This sequence will help prepare you to play a good round of golf and give you a good recharge after your round.

START STRONG

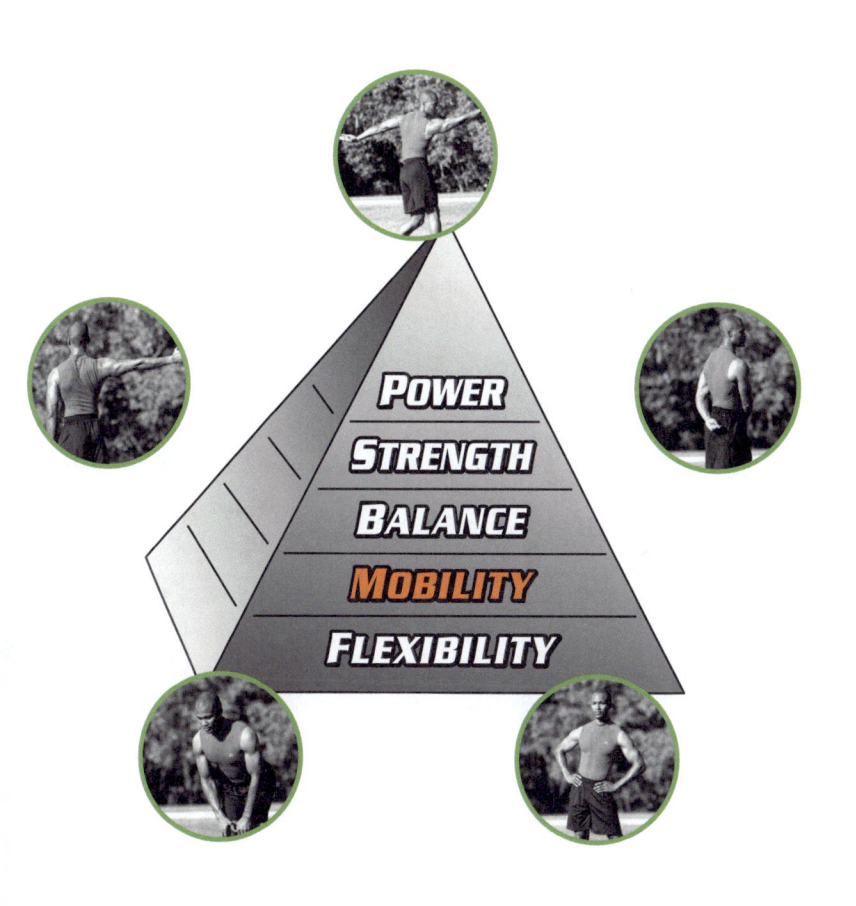

- POWER
- STRENGTH
- BALANCE
- *MOBILITY*
- FLEXIBILITY

1. Egyptian

TARGET AREA: Spine, hips and shoulders
BENEFITS: Improves rotational mobility

The Egyptian, as well as the Kidney Taps (below), were introduced to me by Steve Maxwell, Senior RKC in his DVD *Joint Mobility and Recharge*, and are great mobilizations for the spine, shoulders and hips.

Instructions

1. Stand with your feet shoulder width apart and arms straight out to your sides.
2. Turn your head to the right, your right palm up and your left palm down.
3. At the same time turn your left toe to the right, rotating your left hip inward.
4. Uncoil and repeat the same steps on the other side.
5. Maintain a smooth and steady tempo.

START STRONG

2. Kidney Taps

TARGET AREA: Spine, shoulders, hips, wrists and hands.
BENEFITS: Mobilization and relaxation in the spine, shoulders, hips, hands and wrists

Instructions

1. Stand with feet shoulder width apart.
2. Twist your torso to the right, allowing your arms to swing freely.
3. Allow your right arm to bend naturally and "tap" your lower back or kidney area.
4. Twist in the other direction using the same pattern.
5. Generate the whipping action in the arms by rotation the pivoting with the foot and rotating with the hips and trunk. Relax the arms and let them just enjoy ride.

START STRONG

3. Hip Circles

TARGET AREA: Hip joint
BENEFITS: Mobilizes and increases blood fow to the hip joints

Instructions

1. Stand with your feet shoulder width apart.
2. Place your hands on your hips.
3. Move your hips around an imaginary circle
4. Focus on keeping your head and feet in line with each other.
5. The knees can be either locked or slightly unlocked. The slightly unlocked position has more of a carryover to golf. The locked knee position helps keep the drill exclusive to the hip joint.

START STRONG

4. Knee Circles

TARGET AREA: Knee joint
BENEFITS: Increases mobility and blood flow to the knees

Instructions

1. Stand with your feet together.
2. Place your hands on your knees.
3. Bend your knees and simultaneously move them in a circular fashion. Go down as far as you are able to keep a smooth and comfortable tempo.
4. Reverse the direction of the circle in the middle of your set. If you do 20 reps, change directions on number 10.

START STRONG

5. Neck Trunk Trainer

TARGET AREA: Neck, shoulders, upper and middle back.
BENEFITS: Recharges the upper body during a round of golf; Improves posture, increases spinal rotation and mobility.

This is an excellent pre-golf exercise as it primes all of the rotational reflexes from head to toe. You can also do this one in the middle or end of your round to give you a recharge.

Instructions

1. Stand with your feet shoulder-width apart, with your right arm in front.
2. Sequence 1: Rotate your arm backwards to the right, keeping your eye on your hand. Note how far you can rotate comfortably.
3. Return back to the starting position.
4. Sequence 2: Rotate your right arm back while keeping your head straight and hip square. Do this for 5 reps.
5. Return back to the stating position.
6. Sequence 3: Now rotate your arm back to the right while turning your head to the left. As your head turns left, your eyes will turn right. Focus on keeping your eyes fixed on an object as your head turns. This tip is VERY IMPORTANT as it increases the coordination between your eyes and neck. Remember the gyroscope analogy given in the levator scapulae stretch. Do this 5 times.
7. Sequence 4: Finally repeat your initial full backward rotation and note how much further you can rotate.
8. Repeat steps using the left arm.

NOTE: Please pay close attention to the head and eye positions of this drill. Another benefit of this drill is that is primes the occulo-cervical reflexes or the connection between your eye and neck muscles. This is important, as it will help you keep your eyes on the ball.

START STRONG

5. Neck Trunk Trainer - Sequence 1

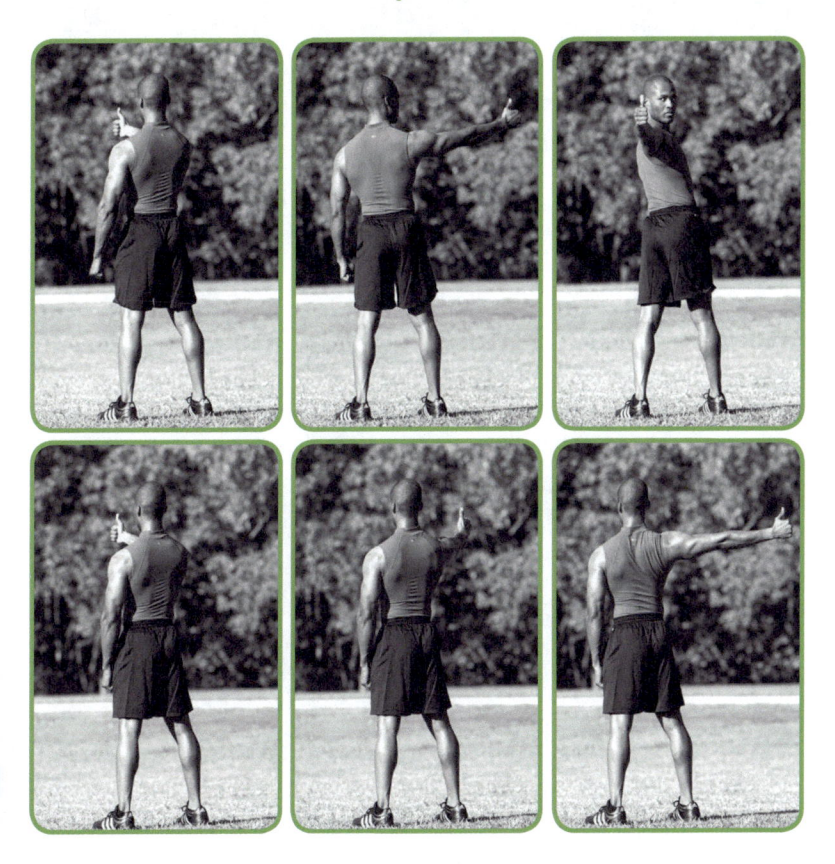

5. Neck Trunk Trainer - Sequence 2

5. Neck Trunk Trainer - Sequence 3

Repetitions for Mobility Exercises

Ideally, you'd perform as many reps as your age. But until you build up the fitness and skill to do this, start with 20 reps and work up from there. Studies have shown that it takes about 30 reps to get an aerobic response in the muscles. An aerobic response means that you have blood flow and oxygen flowing to the muscles and joints. Because of the quick tempo of these drills, you may need to do more. This rules will apply to mobility drills 1-4. Please stick to the 5-5-5 reps scheme for the Neck Truck Trainer.

START STRONG

START STRONG ROUTINE

PHASE II: MOBILITY

TRAINING SCHEDULE

The following is a four-week flexibility and mobility training cycle. Notice the gradual change in training volume (the number of sets and repetitions per exercise) from week to week.

START STRONG

Week 1

1. Stretches – 2 reps each
Swing Simulation – 2 sets of 20 reps

2. Mobility – 2 sets of 20-50 reps
Swing Simulation – 2 sets of 10 reps

3. Stretches – 2 sets each
Swing Simulation – 2 sets of 20 reps

4. Mobility – 2 sets of 20-50 reps
Swing Simulation – 2 sets of 10 reps

5. Stretches – 2 sets each
Swing Simulation – 2 sets of 20 reps

6. Mobility – 2 sets of 20-50 reps
Swing Simulation – 2 sets of 10 reps

7. REST

Week 2

1. Stretches – 3 reps each
Swing Simulation – 3 sets of 20 reps

2. Mobility – 3 sets of 20-50 reps
Swing Simulation – 3 sets of 10 reps

3. Stretches – 3 sets each
Swing Simulation – 3 sets of 20 reps

4. Mobility – 3 sets of 20-50 reps
Swing Simulation – 3 sets of 10 reps

5. Stretches – 3 sets each
Swing Simulation – 3 sets of 20 reps

6. Mobility – 3 sets of 20-50 reps
Swing Simulation – 3 sets of 10 reps

7. REST

NOTE: Swing Simulation means take practice strokes with your golf club. Be very deliberate with your mechanics in all phases:

- Grip
- Set up
- Back swing/Take Away
- Follow through
- Finish

Perform the first 5 reps slow and then gradually work up to full swing speed

Week 3

1. Stretches – 4 reps each
Swing Simulation – 4 sets of 20 reps

2. Mobility – 4 sets of 20-50 reps
Swing Simulation – 4 sets of 10 reps

3. Stretches – 4 sets each
Swing Simulation – 4 sets of 20 reps

4. Mobility – 4 sets of 20-50 reps
Swing Simulation – 4 sets of 10 reps

5. Stretches – 4 sets each
Swing Simulation – 4 sets of 20 reps

6. Mobility – 4 sets of 20-50 reps
Swing Simulation – 4 sets of 10 reps

7. REST

Week 4 (Recovery Week)

Notice the drop in training volume as compared to Week 3? This is called an unloading or recovery period. It's good to do this every 3 to 6 weeks to stay fresh and reduce the likelihood of fatigue-related injuries.

1. Stretches – 2 reps each
Swing Simulation – 2 sets of 20 reps
2. Mobility – 2 sets of 20-50 reps
Swing Simulation – 2 sets of 10 reps
3. Stretches – 2 sets each
Swing Simulation – 2 sets of 20 reps
4. Mobility – 2 sets of 20-50 reps
Swing Simulation – 2 sets of 10 reps
5. Stretches – 2 sets each
Swing Simulation – 2 sets of 20 reps
6. Mobility – 2 sets of 20-50 reps
Swing Simulation – 2 sets of 10 reps
7. REST

START STRONG – PERFORMANCE TRACKER

It's All about the details!

Golf is a game if details. The grip, stance, pace of your swing, weight shift, wind direction, lie of the ball, the terrain and the literally hundreds of other variables that can be considered when trying to play your best golf. If you approach your Start Strong Training with the same level of detail, I PROMISE you that it will correlate to better golf performance. Use the following guidelines to help you monitor your training with the utmost efficiency.

Exercise	Reps Wk1	Reps Wk2	Reps Wk3	Reps Wk4	Duration	Rest
1. Head Rotation						
2. Neck Side Bend						
3. Levator Scap						
4. Trunk Side Bend						
5. Thoracic Mobilization						
6. Kneeling Back Twist						
7. Shoulder Twist						
8. Good Morning Stretch						
9. Cigarette Butt Stretch						
10. Windmill Stretch						
11. Groin Rock						
12. Kneeling Lunge Stretch						

Mobility Drills

Exercise	Reps Wk1	Reps Wk2	Reps Wk3	Reps Wk4	SETS	REST
1. Egyptian						
2. Kidney Taps						
3. Hip Circles						
4. Knee Circles						
5. Neck Trunk Trainer						

NOTES:

* Make notes of the drills that you are having more difficulty executing.
* Record an drills that you find are easy for you as well so that you can spend less
time on those and more time on the more challenging ones.

NOTES:

NOTES:

NOTES:

NOTES:

Conclusion

Congratulations! You now have the tools and techniques for a more powerful, accurate and consistent golf swing. The skills and insight that you now possess, will serve you for the rest of your life both on and off the golf course. As much as I love the game of golf and helping people like yourself play better, my biggest thrill is witnessing how these techniques improve all aspects of my clients' lives.

From the young player looking to land their full ride scholarship, to tour professionals looking to level up their game to rise up the rankings. The 80 year
retired player that can now hit it 50 yards longer because he can move better and is out of pain. It will be an honor to lock arms and help you reach your highest potential as well.

If you like the idea of getting a comprehensive performance evaluation, a customized plan and then deep diving into the Maximum Golf Performance intermediate and advanced trainings, please reach out by emailing us at: golf@terrencethomas.com.

Start Strong...Hit It Long,

Terrence

Bonus Lesson

PEAK PERFORMANCE PRINCIPLES

Discover The 7 Skills For Maximum Golf Performance

Why Did I Write This Report?

Twenty four years ago, I became a golf fitness and performance specialist. This was when golf fitness was just becoming popular thanks to Tiger Woods.

As a lifelong athlete myself, I wanted a way to stay connected to sports and work with people that were high achievers and motivated to improve. Golfers checked all of the boxes.

It also helped that I lived in Florida, the golf capital of the world.

As difficult of a game as golf is, 24 years of experience has shown me that there is massive opportunity for golfers to make shocking improvements in their golf swing...and do it lightning fast!

Peak Performance For All Levels

This applies to the pro that's looking to climb the money board and win a major...

All the way to the C suite executive that just wants to get the ball around the course and not embarrass themselves.

When you understand a few basic principles, you will be able to add yards of accurate distance to your golf swing and do it easier and faster than you ever thought possible.

The mistake that I see golfers make when trying to hit the ball farther is they make it way more complicated than it needs to be.

Golf is a game of controlled power and to make a controlled power move, it takes more precision than brute force.

I want you to get the most out of your investment of time and money when it comes to improving your golf swing and playing better on the course.

This is why I wrote this report to help you do just that.

Let's get started.

I. Proper Grip:

The grip is the foundation of your golf swing. It directly affects your clubface control, power transfer, and overall swing mechanics. To fix power leaks in your golf swing, it's crucial to develop a proper grip. Here are the key elements to consider:

1. **Hand Placement:** Start by placing the club handle diagonally across your fingers. The club should run from the base of the pinky finger to the middle of the index finger. This neutral grip allows for greater control and power.

2. **Pressure Points:** Apply pressure with your top hand (left hand for right-handed players, right hand for left-handed players) primarily in the last three fingers. The pressure in your bottom hand should be more evenly distributed across the fingers.

3. **Finger Alignment:** Ensure that your fingers are aligned properly on the club. They should wrap around the grip comfortably, without overlapping or excessive tension. This allows for a relaxed but secure grip.

4. **Hand Position:** The position of your hands on the club plays a significant role in the swing's power generation. For a standard grip, the "V" shape formed by the thumb and index finger of your top hand should point toward your right shoulder (for right-handed players). The bottom hand's "V" shape should point toward your right ear.

5. **Thumb Placement:** The placement of your thumbs can influence clubface control. Keep your thumbs running straight down the grip or slightly to the right (for right-handed players). This helps prevent excessive wrist movement and promotes a solid impact position.

6. **Rehearse and Assess:** Spend time rehearsing your grip and checking it regularly. Take note of any tendencies to grip the club too tightly or with improper hand positions. Regular assessment helps you maintain a consistent grip.

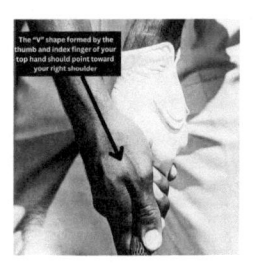

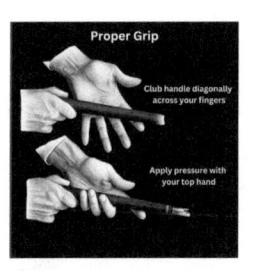

TIPS TO PRACTICE YOUR GRIP:

1. Mirror Drills: Stand in front of a mirror and rehearse your grip. Pay attention to the positioning of your hands and fingers. This visual feedback will help you refine your grip.

2. Grip Pressure: Experiment with grip pressure to find the right balance. Start with a moderate grip pressure, and avoid squeezing the club too tightly. This allows for better feel and control.

3. Awareness During Swings: During your practice sessions, focus on maintaining the proper grip throughout your swings. Regularly check your grip to ensure it hasn't slipped or changed position.

V. Lag and Release:

Creating and maintaining lag in your golf swing and executing a proper release is crucial for generating power and fixing power leaks. Lag refers to the angle formed between the club shaft and your lead arm during the downswing. It allows for the storage and release of energy, resulting in increased clubhead speed and distance. Here's how you can work on lag and release:

1. **Wrist Hinge:** During the backswing, focus on hinging your wrists naturally. Allow the clubhead to move up while maintaining a straight lead arm. This wrist hinge sets the stage for generating lag during the downswing.

2. **Downswing Transition:** As you initiate the downswing, strive for a smooth and controlled transition. Avoid casting or releasing the club too early, as it can lead to power leaks. Instead, maintain the angle between the club shaft and your lead arm as you start the downswing.

3. **Late Release:** Aim to release the club late in the downswing, just before impact. This delayed release helps maximize the clubhead speed and ensures proper energy transfer to the ball.

4. **Maintain Wrist Cock:** Throughout the downswing, focus on maintaining the wrist cock and lag angle. This creates a whipping motion, increasing the clubhead speed at impact.

5. **Active Hands:** Engage your hands actively in the downswing to maintain the lag. Avoid any excessive tension or gripping pressure, as it can inhibit the natural release of the club.

6. **Release and Extension:** Just before impact, allow your wrists to release naturally, allowing the clubhead to catch up with your hands. Simultaneously, extend your arms fully for maximum power and a solid strike.

Lag & Release

Aim to release the club late in the downswing, just before impact

Wrist Hinge

Initiate the downswing with a bump of the hips towards the target.

V. Lag and Release:

TO PRACTICE LAG AND RELEASE:

1. **Lag Drills:** Practice drills that help you develop and feel the lag in your swing. For example, the "Pump Drill" involves rehearsing the transition and downswing while focusing on maintaining the angle between the club shaft and your lead arm. This drill encourages the feeling of a late release.

2. **Impact Bag Training:** Incorporate impact bag training into your practice routine. Strike the bag with a focus on maintaining lag and achieving a crisp impact position. The bag provides feedback and helps you develop the proper release.

3. **Slow Motion Swings:** Practice slow-motion swings to develop a better feel for the lag and release. Pay close attention to the position of your wrists and the clubshaft during the downswing. Gradually increase the speed as you gain more control and understanding of the lag.

4. **Visualization:** Visualize a crisp release and a powerful strike as you practice. Mentally rehearse the feeling of maintaining the lag and releasing the club at the right moment. This visualization technique helps reinforce the proper mechanics.

VI. Timing and Tempo:

The timing and tempo of your golf swing have a significant impact on power generation and overall swing efficiency. By developing a smooth and consistent rhythm, you can fix power leaks and achieve better results. Here's how you can improve your timing and tempo:

1. **Establish a Pre-shot Routine:** Develop a pre-shot routine that helps you find a comfortable and consistent tempo. This routine may involve taking a few practice swings or visualizing your desired shot. A consistent pre-shot routine helps set the tone for your swing and establishes a steady tempo.

2. **One-Piece Takeaway:** During the initial stages of the backswing, aim for a synchronized and connected movement of your hands, arms, and shoulders. This one-piece takeaway promotes a smooth transition and better timing.

3. **Pause at the Top:** At the top of your backswing, briefly pause to create a sense of rhythm and control. This pause allows you to gather your thoughts and prepare for the downswing. Avoid any excessive hesitation or lengthy pauses that disrupt the flow of your swing.

4. **Smooth Transition:** Focus on making a seamless transition from the backswing to the downswing. Avoid abrupt or jerky movements that can lead to timing issues. Practice transitioning with a gradual shift of weight and a smooth rotation of your body.

5. **Find Your Tempo:** Experiment with different tempos to find the one that suit your swing best. Some golfers benefit from a slower, deliberate tempo, while others find success with a faster pace. Discover the rhythm that allows you to maintain control and generate power effectively.

VII. Golf Strength Development:

Golf is a sport that demands a unique combination of strength, flexibility, balance, and coordination. To optimize performance and reduce the risk of injury, golfers must develop various types of strength, each contributing to different aspects of the golf swing and overall physical health. This summary delves into the key types of strength essential for golf: core strength, rotational strength, upper body strength, lower body strength, and functional strength.

Core strength is fundamental to a powerful and efficient golf swing. The core muscles, including the abdominals, obliques, lower back, and pelvic muscles, stabilize the spine and pelvis, allowing for controlled and explosive movements. A strong core enables golfers to maintain proper posture throughout the swing, reducing the risk of lower back injuries. Exercises such as planks, Russian twists, and medicine ball throws are effective for developing core strength. Stability ball exercises can also enhance core stability, crucial for maintaining balance during the swing.

Rotational strength is specifically important for generating power in the golf swing. The golf swing is a complex rotational movement that involves the entire body, from the feet to the hands. Strength in the muscles responsible for rotation—such as the obliques, transverse abdominis, and the muscles around the hips and shoulders—is crucial. Exercises that enhance rotational strength include woodchoppers, cable rotations, and rotational medicine ball throws. These exercises mimic the twisting motion of the golf swing, thereby improving the power and control of this movement.

Upper body strength contributes significantly to the control and power of the golf swing. The shoulders, chest, and arms play vital roles in the different phases of the swing, from the takeaway to the follow-through. Strong shoulders and arms help in maintaining the club's position and generating clubhead speed. Key exercises include push-ups, pull-ups, dumbbell presses, and rows. Additionally, shoulder stability exercises, such as scapular retractions and rotator cuff strengthening, are essential to prevent injuries and ensure smooth, controlled swings.

Lower body strength provides the foundation for the golf swing, with the legs and hips generating much of the power and stability needed. Strong glutes, quadriceps, hamstrings, and calves help in maintaining balance, controlling the downswing, and ensuring a solid impact with the ball. Squats, lunges, deadlifts, and calf raises are excellent for building lower body strength. Plyometric exercises like box jumps and lateral bounds can enhance explosive power, which translates into greater driving distance. Moreover, hip mobility and strength exercises, such as hip bridges and clamshells, support better rotation and reduce the risk of hip injuries.

Functional strength refers to the ability to perform movements that mimic the demands of the sport, thereby improving overall performance and reducing the risk of injury. For golfers, functional strength training focuses on integrating various types of strength into movements that simulate the golf swing. Compound exercises, such as kettlebell swings, Turkish get-ups, and full-body cable exercises, are beneficial. These exercises train multiple muscle groups simultaneously, improving coordination and muscle synergy. Balance and stability exercises, like single-leg deadlifts and stability ball exercises, are also crucial for developing functional strength.

VII. Golf Strength Development:

- **Core strength**
- **Functional Strength**
- **Rotational Strength**
- **Lower Body Strength**
- **Upper Body Strength**

WHAT'S NEXT?
Join The P.A.C.K.

Power Accuracy Consistency Knowledge

The Maximum Golf Performance Pack (MGPP) is a comprehensive 12-month program designed to enhance golfers' clubhead speed, power, distance, and accuracy. Each month focuses on specific elements of golf fitness, integrating strength training, flexibility exercises, swing mechanics, and mental conditioning. The program combines personalized fitness routines with advanced golf techniques and educational components.

- Fitness
- Equipment
- Nutrition
- Instruction
- Swing Mechanics
- Technology
- Community
- Training Aids

MAXIMUM GOLF PERFORMANCE

Structured Month-by-Month Curriculum

- 11-12: PEAK PERFORMANCE INTEGRATION
- 9-10: PRECISION AND ACCURACY
- 7-8: ENHANCING CONSISTENCY
- 5-6: POWER DEVELOPMENT
- 3-4: BUILDING STRENGTH AND FLEXIBILITY
- 1-2: FOUNDATION AND BASELINE DEVELOPMENT

Training Aids, Equipment and Coaching

You'll not only enhance your golf game with a structured, scientifically-backed program but also receive top-tier bonuses to support your journey towards peak performance.

For more information about enrollment go to www.maximumgolf.net/pack

Level Up Your Game

Swing Accelerator Coaching

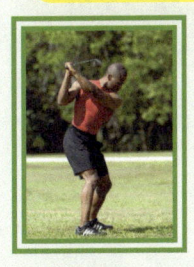

Swing Analysis

Send a video of your golf swing (down the line and top of head).

Golf Swing Performance Plan

I'll send you a customized lesson with swing performance drills.

Virtual Coaching Sessions

3 coaching sessions to guarantee that your form is perfect and you are on trac.

Scan QR Code To Register

Level Up Your Game

Made in the USA
Columbia, SC
20 September 2024